1000

First Words
in Spanish

Learning Spanish

Learning a new language is fun. The best way to learn Spanish is to go to a country where it is spoken all around you. Talking with someone who knows the language very well is good, too. If possible, share this book with a grown-up who will help you pronounce the words properly and ask you the questions under each picture.

Spanish is not a difficult language to learn, but you will notice some things about it that are different from English.

In English, there is only one word for **the**. We say **the house** and **the hat**. In Spanish, there are two different words—**la casa** and **el sombrero**. If you are talking about more than one thing, instead of **the houses** and **the hats**, you say **las casas** and **los sombreros**. Each time you learn a new word in Spanish, try to learn the word for **the** that goes with it.

In the same way, **a house** and **a hat** are **una casa** and **un sombrero**. **Some houses** and **some hats** are **unas casas** and **unos sombreros**.

You may also notice that some Spanish words have little signs above the letters. These help you pronounce the word in the right way.

Have fun learning Spanish!

1000

First Words
in Spanish

Written by Nicola Baxter and Sam Budds

Illustrated by Susie Lacome

ARMADILLO

© 2001 Bookmart Limited

All rights reserved. No part of this publication may be
reproduced, stored in a retrieval system or transmitted
by any means, electronic, mechanical, photocopying or
otherwise, without the prior permission of the publisher.

Published by Armadillo Books
an imprint of
Bookmart Limited
Registered Number 2372865
Trading as Bookmart Limited
Desford Road
Enderby
Leicester
LE9 5AD

ISBN 1 90046 684 8

Produced for Bookmart Limited by Nicola Baxter
PO Box 215
Framingham Earl
Norwich
NR14 7UR

Editorial consultant: Ronne Randall
Designer: Amanda Hawkes

Printed in Indonesia

Índice

En Casa

el cubo
de basura

el cubo

la caja
de herramientas

la jardinera
de ventana

el tejado

el caño

la senda

la chimenea

la escalera

la ventana

la puerta

Who is in the garage?
Is the bucket blue?
Can you see two gloves?
Where are Teddy Bear's boots?

6

 la radio

 el umbral

 el termo

 la caja de comida

 los ladrillos

 la teja

 la espaldera

 la luz de seguridad

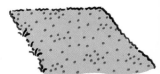 la calzada

 el timbre

 la servilleta

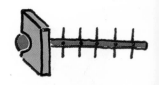 el aéreo

 el guante

¿Quién está en el garaje?
¿Es el cubo azul?
¿Puedes ver dos guantes?
¿Dónde están las botas del Osito?

La Cocina

el jarro la cacerola el libro de cocina

el tostador

el rodillo de cocina

el tarro

el frigorífico

la cuchara de palo

el sartén

el trapo de cocina

el micro-onda

What is on the counter?
Can you see the lid for the saucepan?
Who is looking in the fridge?
What could you use for mixing?

8

la tabla

el taburete

la cocina
eléctrica

el calentador
de agua

la plancha

el fregadero

la mezcladora

el jabón
de fregar

el cajón

el tablón
de anuncios

el lavaplatos

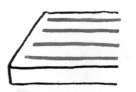
el escurreplatos

la escudilla

¿Qué hay en la tabla?
¿Puedes ver la cobertera del sartén?
¿Quién está mirando en el frigorífico?
¿Qué usas para mezclar?

9

El Dormitorio

 el cepillo   la colcha   el pendiente    el peine

la cama

el armario

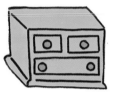
la cómoda

la mesita
de noche

el pijama

el batín

la almohada

What can you see in Teddy Bear's bedroom?
What is under the bedside table?
What color are Teddy Bear's pajamas?
What is on the night table?

10

las
zapatillas

los calcetines

el baúl

el póster

la cometa

el tebeo

la luz

la tabla
de estatura

la papelera

el reloj

el dibujo

la percha

la hucha

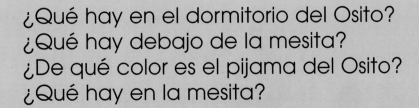
¿Qué hay en el dormitorio del Osito?
¿Qué hay debajo de la mesita?
¿De qué color es el pijama del Osito?
¿Qué hay en la mesita?

El Cuarto de Baño

el jabón

el paño

la esponja

el cepillo
de dientes

el baño

el lavabo

el papel higiénico

la ducha

la cortina
de ducha

la estera de baño

el armario

What color are the wall tiles?
What is on the bath mat?
How many toothbrushes can you see?
How many pawprints can you find?

 el váter

 el espejo

 el cepillo

 el grifo

 la balanza

la toalla

 el champú

 el jabón de baño

 la pasta de dientes

 el barco

 los azulejos

 el cepillo de espalda

 el pato

¿De qué color son los azulejos?
¿Qué hay en la estera de baño?
¿Cuántos cepillos de dientes hay?
¿Cuántas huellas de patas hay?

El Salón

el reloj

la cortina

la lámpara

el cojín

la alfombra

la butaca

la estantería

la revista

el aspirador

la planta

el trapo de polvo

What is on the sofa?
How many dust cloths can you see?
What is on the bookcase?
What color is the armchair?

el periódico

el vaso
de flores

el vídeo

la foto

la maqueta

la obra

la mesa

el tele control

el sofá

la chimenea

la televisión

el estéreo

el papel
de paredes

¿Qué hay en la sofá?
¿Cuántos trapos de polvo hay?
¿Qué hay en la estantería?
¿De qué color es la butaca?

15

El Desván

 la cuna

 la casa de muñecas

 la jaula

 el tragaluz

 el cartón

 el cuadro

 la maleta

 el maniquí

 el patín

 la bombilla

 la telaraña

How many jars can you see?
What is on the sled?
Can you see a bed?
What is red and white?

el bote
de pintura

la tumbona

las botellas

el
sombrero de paja

los tarros

la escotilla

la caña

la mecedora

los adornos

la máquina
de coser

el caballo
de balancín

los botes
del patinaje

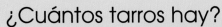
el trineo

¿Cuántos tarros hay?
¿Qué hay sobre el trineo?
¿Puedes ver una cama?
¿Qué hay de rojo y blanco?

El Jardín

 la horca

 la césped

el cortacesped

las semillas

 la carretilla

 las tijeras de jardín

 la tierra

 la pala

 la maceta

 la regadera

 la manga

What is on the grass?
What is in the wheelbarrow?
How many birds can you see?
What color is the watering can?

los hojas

el nido

la azada

la horca
del mano

la paleta

la mesita
de pájaros

el cobertizo

la cesta
de plantas

el rastrillo

el seto

las flores

el baño de
pájaros

la escoba

¿Qué hay sobre la césped?
¿Qué hay en la caretilla?
¿Cuántos pájaros hay?
¿De qué color es la regadera?

La Calle

 la bicicleta

 la paloma

 los caramelos

 el pastel

 la acera

 la verja

 la farola

 la papelera

 la furgoneta

 el conductor

 la silleta

How many wheels can you see?
Which shop sells lollipops?
What color are the boots in the shoe shop?
Do you like cakes?

20

 el colegio

 la panadería

 el paquete

 la calle

 el piruí

 la boca de alcantarilla

el casco

 la bolsa

 la zapatería

 el poste indicador

 la bombonería

 la cuerda de saltar

 las botas

La Calle Mayor

¿Cuántas ruedas hay?
¿Cuál de las tiendas venden los pirulís?
¿De qué color son las botas en la zapatería?
¿A ti, te gusta los pasteles?

21

El Supermercado

el
monedero

el dinero

la fruta

el bolso

las latas

el comprador

el carro

la cola

la cesta

la bolsa

la caja

How many bears are in the line?
Can you see Teddy Bear?
Where is the milk?
What is on the conveyor belt?

la leche

las llaves

el yogur

el cartón

el zumo

la miel

el código

la dependienta

el recibo

el signo

el cajero

los legumbres

¿Cuántos osos están en la cola?
¿Puedes ver el Osito?
¿Dónde está la leche?
¿Qué hay en la cinta transportadora?

la cinta
transportadora

23

La Escuela

 la profesora

 los rotuladores

 el papel

el tarro de agua

 la regla

 la pizarra

 el mapa

 los coloretes

 la arcilla

 la tiza

  la percha

What is the teacher holding?
What do you need for painting?
How many pupils can you see?
What color is the ruler?

el alumno

el pincel

la goma

el dibujo

la pecera

el cabellete

las pinturas

el alfabeto

el cuaderno

el ordenador

el bolso

el rompecabezas

las tijeras

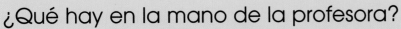

¿Qué hay en la mano de la profesora?
¿Qué necesitas para hacer la pintura?
¿Cuántos alumnos hay?
¿De qué color es la regla?

El Transporte

el helicoptero

el globo

el cohete

el paracaída

el autocár

el coche

el camión de averías

la caravana

el carro

el coche clásico

el tándem

la escavadora

Can you see Teddy Bear?
What color is the garbage truck?
Which car is very old?
How many cars can you see?

el coche de carreras

la apisonadora

el furgón de basura

el camión

el gokart

la furgoneta

la moto

el camión de gasolina

la escavadora

la transportadora de coches

el furgón

¿Dónde está el Osito?
¿De qué color es el furgón de basura?
¿Cuál de los coches es muy viejo?
¿Cuántos coches hay?

La Granja

 la cordera

 la oveja

 el cerdo

 el cerdito

los pollitos

la gallina

el perro

el caballo

el potro

el granjero

la granja

Where is the duck?
What is the farmer holding?
How many chicks does he have?
Is the tractor yellow?

el pato

el patito

el gato

la rata

la puerta
de verja

la valla

el espanta
pájaros

el estanque

el gallo

la vaca

el ternero

el campo

¿Dónde está la pata?
¿Qué lleva el granjero?
¿Cuántos pollitos hay?
¿Es amarillo, el tractór?

el tractór

29

El Parque

 el banco

 la rodillera

 el pájaro

 la sirena

el helado

el tobogán

los columpios

el corredor

el hoyo de arena

la fuente

el macizo de flores

Is Teddy Bear on the swing?
What is in the picnic basket?
How many bears are wearing helmets?
How many wheels does a tricycle have?

 el triciclo

 el monopatín

 el subibaja

 las ruedas

 el cesto

 el arco

 la pelota

 el picnic

 la ardilla

 los bocadillos

 el patinete

 los pátines

 el estereo personal

¿Está el Osito en el columpios?

¿Qué hay en el cesto?

¿Cuántos de los osos llevan los cascos?

¿Cuántas ruedas tienen el triciclo?

El Mundo de Libros

la varilla de virtudes

el fuente
de deseos

el hongo

el elfo

el hada

la lanza

el escudo

la corona

la espada

la armadura

el dragón

el caballero   la princesa

Who can do magic?
What color is the dragon?
Where does a king live?
Who wears armor?

la bandana

el sombrero de copa

el paje · la calabaza

el mágico

la capa

el príncipe · la reina · el rey

el gigante · el castillo

¿Quién hace el mágico?
¿De qué color es el dragón?
¿Dónde vive el rey?
¿Quién lleva la armadura?

El Campo

las tiendas de campaña

el árbol

el paseante

el puente

el bosque

la montaña

el campo

el río

el lago

la rama

la hoguera

How many cars does the train have?
Who is sitting on a log?
Is the sleeping bag in the tent?
Is the rowboat on the river?

el tronco

 el tren

 el vagón

 el arbusto

 los gemelos

 la cascada

 los troncos

el pueblo

la vía

el bote de remos

la colina

el saco de dormir

las rocas

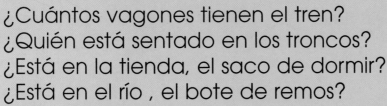

¿Cuántos vagones tienen el tren?

¿Quién está sentado en los troncos?

¿Está en la tienda, el saco de dormir?

¿Está en el río , el bote de remos?

35

El Puerto

la pez

el canalete

la cuerda

la boya

la portilla

el submarino

el transatlántico

el pescador

la grúa

el pescadero

el barco
de motor

What can go under the water?
What are round windows on a boat called?
How many fish can you see?
What is on the jetty?

36

el chaleco
salvavidas

el gancho

la áncora

la langosta

el mástil

la canoa

el esquiador
acuático

la langostera

el traje de baño

el embarcadero

el buque

el saltador

la guindola

¿Qué va debajo del mar?

¿Cómo se llama las ventanas redondas de un barco?

¿Cuántos peces hay?

¿Qué hay en el embarcadero?

El Aeropuerto

 los servicios  el hangar la etiqueta el tablón

el bastón

el batido

el caro

las llegadas

el autobús

el avión

la torre
de control

How many suitcases can you see?
Who is carrying a mop?
Can you see our Teddy Bear?
Have you ever been in an airplane?

la maleta

 el café

 la pista de aterrizaje

 el fregasuelos

 la limpiadora

 los billetes

 la máquina de fotos

 la mango

 el piloto

 el puente de control

 la azafata

 la mochila

 el teléfono

¿Cuántas maletas hay?
¿Quién lleva un fregasuelos?
¿Dónde está nuestro Osito?
¿Has viajado en un avión?

El Hospital

la bandeja

la enfermera

el vaso
de agua

la venda

la sabana

el médico

el camisón

la medicina

el visitante

las muletas

el algodón

What is the nurse holding?
Who is in the elevator?
Is the doctor's coat red?
Have you ever been in the hospital?

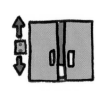 el ascensor

 el portero

 el reloj

 el cabestrillo

 la tirita

 la jeringa

 la manta

 la tarjeta

 la escayola

 la tabla de temperatura

 el estetoscopio

 el termómetro

 la silla de ruedas

¿Qué tiene la enfermera?
¿Quién está en el ascensor?
¿Es rojo, la chaqueta del médico?
¿Has estado una vez en el hospital?

El Mar

la bandera
de pirata

el caballito
de mar

la cadena

la perla

la ballena

el galeón

el mensaje
de botella

el tiburón

el nadador

el cajón

la medusa

What is on the island?
What is in the water?
What goes in a keyhole?
Which is the biggest animal in the ocean?

 el coral

 el pulpo

 el pirata

 el delfín

 la pistola

el pedazo
del ojo

la ostra

 la mapa

 el agujero
de llave

 la isla

 las algas

 la sirena

 la palmera

¿Qué hay en la isla?
¿Qué hay en el mar?
¿Qué va en el agujero de llave?
En el mar, ¿cuál es el animal más grande?

43

La Juguetería

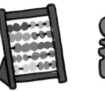 el ábaco

 el juego de bolos

 el castillo

la muñeca

el servicio de té

la caja sorpresa

las pinturas

la peonza

la casa
de muñecas

el juego

el títere

How many blocks can you see?
Who is holding a puppet?
Which toys are for babies?
Which is your favorite toy?

 el collar

 la caretilla

 el yoyo

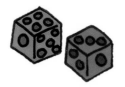 los dados

 las carnicas

 el robot

 las tazitas

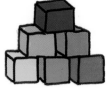 los cubos

 la jugueta de bébés

 los solditos

 el libro de colores

 el coche

 la disfraz

¿Cuántos cubos hay?
¿Quién lleva un títere?
¿Cuáles de los juguetes son para los bébés?
¿Cuál es tú juguete preferido?

45

El Taller

la llave
de tuercas

la lámpara
de bolsillo

la taza

el taladero

el bolsillo

el calendario

el estante

el pomo
de puerta

el metro

las galletas

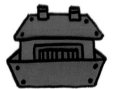
la Arca de Noé

How many animals can you see?
What is on the workbench?
What is on the shelf?
What color is the door?

 la sierra

 el destornillador

 los tornillos

 los clavos

 el martillo

 los anteojos

 la navaja

 el papel de lija

 el mazo

 el tablón

 los animales

 los alicates

 la mesa de trabajo

¿Cuántos animales hay?
¿Qué hay en la mesa de trabajo?
¿Qué hay en el estante?
¿De qué color es la puerta?

47

La Playa

 la bandera

 la arena

 la concha de mar

 el mar

 el castillo de arena

 la estrella de mar

 el bañador

 la sombrilla

 las pierdrecitas

 la red

 las gafas de sol

How many legs does a starfish have?
How many sea shells can you see?
What is very cold?
What color is the flag?

 el cangrejo

 las aletas

 el barco de yate

 los brazales

 el sol

 las olas

 la crema bronceadora

 el faro

 el aro de goma

 la pelota

 el traje de baño

 la gaviota

 el helado

¿Cuántos brazos tiene la estrella de mar?
¿Cuántas conchas hay?
¿Hay algo que es muy frío?
¿De qué color es la bandera?

La Fiesta

 el regalo

 el payaso

 la vela

 el botón

la pajita

el sombrero
de fiesta

la ración
de la tarta

la gaseosa

la taza de papel

el mantel

la tarta

How old is the birthday bear?
How old are you?
How many balloons can you see?
Who is under the table?

50

 el chaleco

 la cinta   el globo

 la corbata de lazo

 la máscara

 el lazo

la venda

 el papel

 la guirnalda de papel

 el bolsito de fiesta

 el sobre

 la tarjeta

 el vestido

¿Cuántos años tiene el osito?
¿Cuántos años tienes tú?
¿Cuántos globos hay?
¿Quién etsá debajo de la mesa?

El Cuerpo

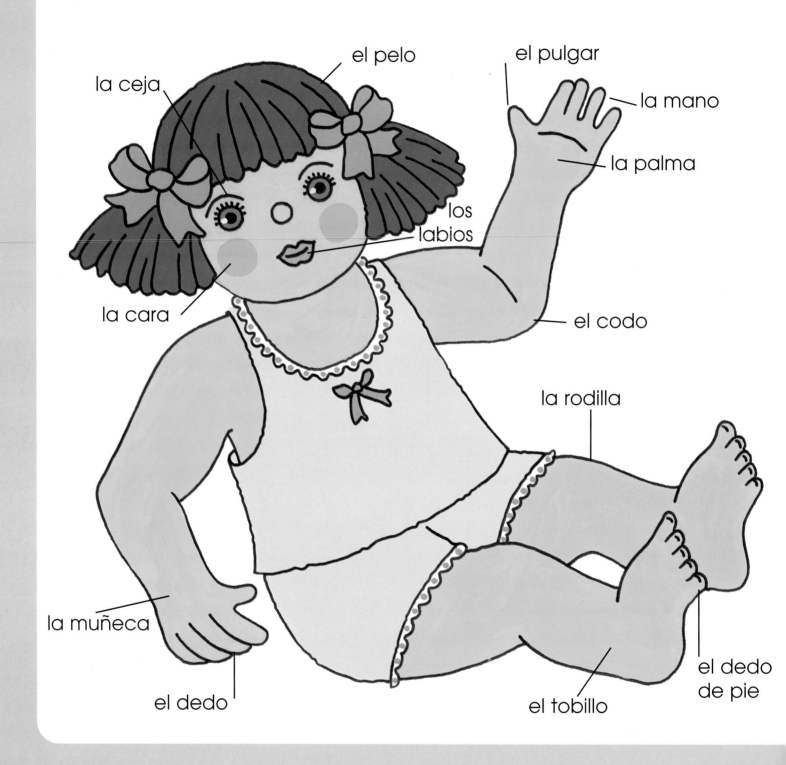

el pelo

la ceja

el pulgar

la mano

la palma

los labios

la cara

el codo

la rodilla

la muñeca

el dedo

el tobillo

el dedo de pie

How many toes does Dolly have?
What color is her hair?
Do you have paws?
Are your eyes blue like Teddy's?

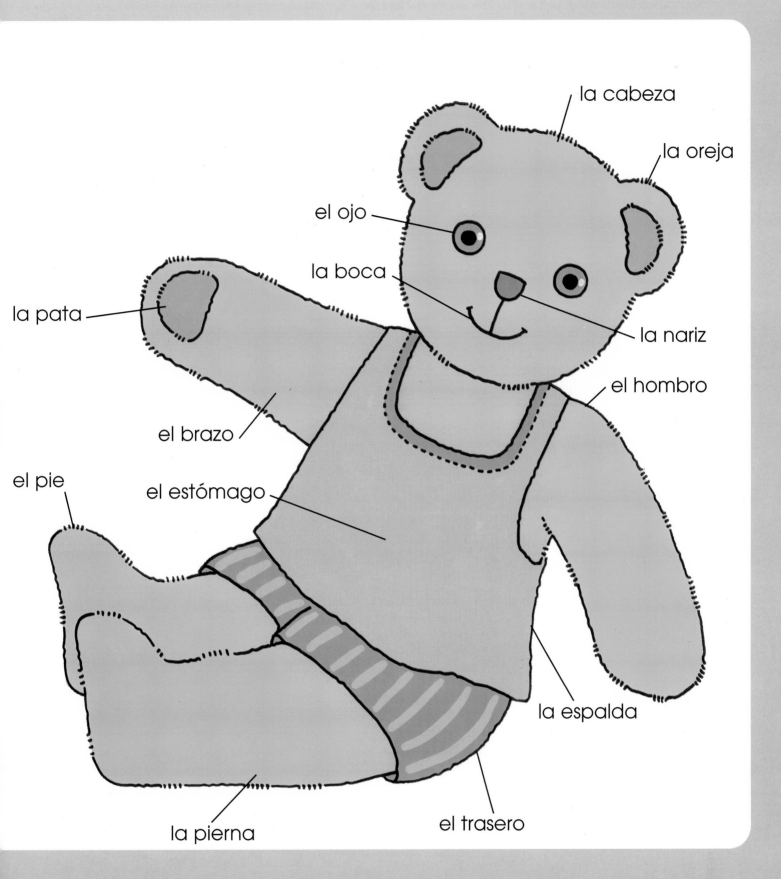

la cabeza

la oreja

el ojo

la boca

la pata

la nariz

el hombro

el brazo

el pie

el estómago

la espalda

la pierna

el trasero

¿Cuántos dedos de pie tiene la muñeca?
¿De qué color es su pelo?
¿Tienes patas?
¿Tienes los ojos azules como el Osito?

Haciendo Cosas

gatear

sentar

leer

abrazar

cantar

beber

comer

escribir

agitar el brazo

lavarse

secarse

dormir

What do you like to do?
What is Teddy Bear doing?
What do babies like doing?
Are you sitting or standing?

dar un puntapié   saltar   montar la bicicleta   saltar

andar   poner la ropa   correr   saltar

empujar   tirar   bailar   esperar

¿Qué te gusta hacer?
¿Qué hace el Osito?
¿Qué les gustan hacer los bébés?
¿Estás sentado o levantado?

la primervera

el verano

el otoño

el invierno

Las Estaciones

Which season is it now?
Is there snow in the summer?
When does Teddy Bear fly his kite?
What comes from clouds?

El Tiempo

el sol

la nieve

el arco de iris

el helado

el ventarrón

los carámbanos

el viento

el copo de nieve

el nube

el tornado

el hombre de nieve

la lluvia

el rocío

el relámpago

el

la inundación

la helada

la niebla

el frío

los charcos

¿En qué estación del año estamos ahora?
¿Hay nieve en el verano?
¿Cuándo lanza su cometa, el Osito?
¿Qué viene de los nubes?

La Comida Preferida

la mantequilla

la galleta

los cereales

el azúcar

la sopa

el perrito caliente

las patatas fritas

la salsa

el chocolate

el arroz

los churros

los espaguetis

What is your favorite food?
Do you like cheese?
How many spoons can you see?
What is on Teddy Bear's ears?

la ensalada

la hamburguesa

la pizza

las judías asadas

el pastel

el queso

el pan

la salchicha

las nueces

la harina

la tortilla

la tarta

¿Cuál es tu comida preferida?
¿A ti, te gusta el queso?
¿Cuántas cucharas hay?
¿Qué hay en las orejas del Osito?

Los Deportes

el criquet

el béisbol

el fútbol americano

el tenis

la salta alta

el tiro con arco

la carrera de tres piernas

la escaleda

la natación

el salto con pértiga

el equipo

la gimnasia

Can you see Teddy Bear?
Which sports need a ball?
Which is your favorite sport?
How many bears are waving?

el salto de
trampolín

el ciclismo

el levantamiento
de pesos

el piragüismo

el patinaje
de ruedas

el golf

el fútbol

la carrera
de bolsas

el patinaje

el baloncesto

el judo

la copa

¿Puedes ver el Osito?
¿Cuál de los deportes necesitan una pelota?
¿Cuál es tu deporte preferido?
¿Cuántos de los osos están agitando los brazos?

La Música

la pandereta

el tríangulo

los platillos

las maracas

el violín

el teclado de música

el trombón

la flauta de pico

el atril

las notas

el director

el violoncelo

Can you play these instruments?
Which instruments do you blow?
Which instruments have strings?
Which instruments do you hit?

la flauta

la música

el oboe

la trompeta

el saxafón

el banjo

el xilofón

la guitarra

la harpa

el piano

los tímpanos

¿Tocas algunos de estos instrumentos?
¿Cuáles de los instrumentos soplas?
¿Cuáles de los instrumentos tienen cuerdas?
¿Cuáles de los instrumentos tienes que golpear?

Los Bébés

 el sonajero el babero   el biberón   el chupete

las botas de lana

el monitor

el colchón de cambiante

el libro de bébé

la hucha

la camiseta de dormir

la camita

Do baby bears sleep in a big bed?
What color is the training cup?
What are the baby bears wearing?
Do you have a piggy bank?

el cochecito

el chal

el pañal

el tisú

el chupador

el orinal

la silla alta

la tazita

el libro de tela

el libro de cartón

el juguete mimosa

el colchón

el bolso de bébés

¿Duermen en una cama grande los ositos?
¿De qué color es la tazita?
¿Qué llevan los ositos?
¿Tienes una hucha?

Los Números

una casa

dos coches

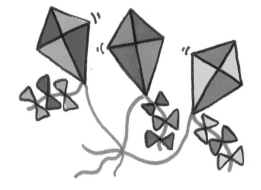
tres cometas

cuatro conéjos

cinco globos

seis patas

siete fresas

ocho coloretes

nueve flores

diez corozones

What color are the rabbits?
How many bears can you see?
How many flowers can you count?
What is five plus seven?

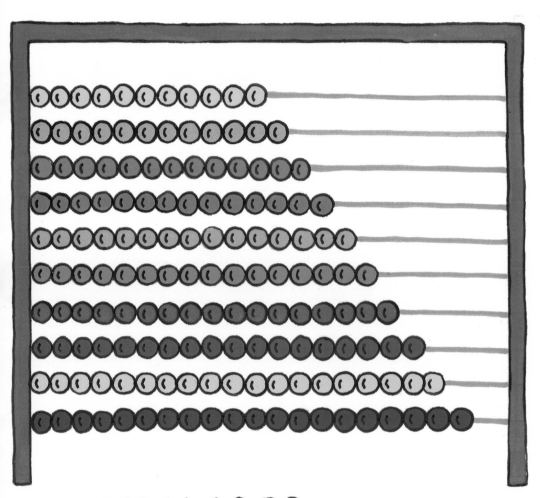

11 once
12 doce
13 trece
14 catorce
15 quince
16 dieciseis
17 diecisiete
18 dieciocho
19 diecinueve
20 veinte

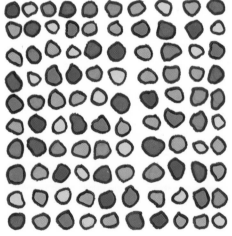

cien

tecero segundo primero

¿De qué color son los conejos?
¿Cuántos osos hay?
¿Cuántos flores hay?
Suma cinco y siete.

Los Colores

 azul 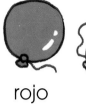 rojo  gris rosa  verde

 blanco

 negro

 amarillo

 marrón

 violeta

 naranja

 azul oscurro

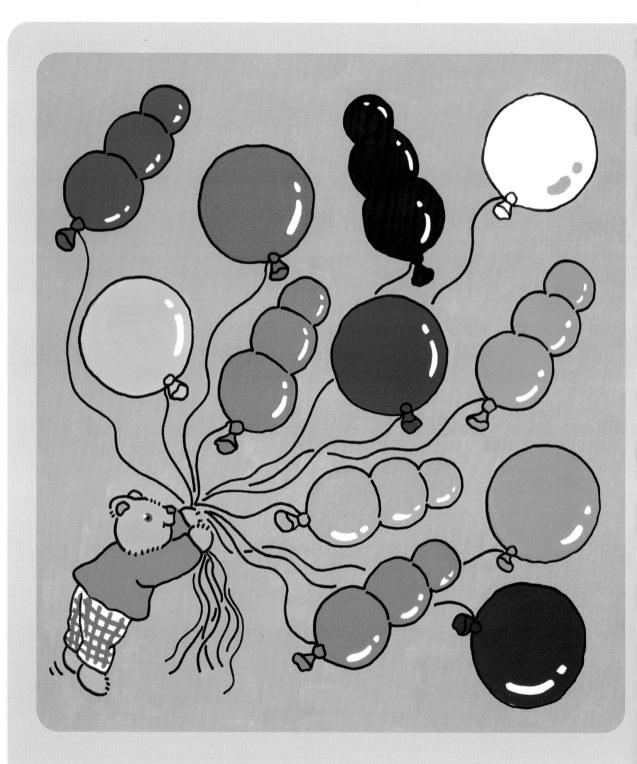

What is your favorite color?
What color is Teddy Bear's top?
Are there zigzags on Teddy Bear's pants?
Which shape is pink?

Las Formas

la
corazón

las rayas

el circulo

el
cuadro

la
estrella

el diamante

el rectangulo

los zig zag

los puntos

la ovalada

el triangulo

los cuadrados

¿Cuál es tu color preferido?
¿De qué color es el jersey del Osito?
¿Hay los zig zag en los pantalones del Osito?
¿Cuál de las formas es de color rosa?

69

La Ropa

 el sombrero   el panuelo   los guantes  las zapatillas de deporte

la bufunda

los vaqueros

la chaqueta

la blusa

la camiseta

los pantalones

el suéter

What do you wear on a hot day?
What do you wear on a cold day?
What color are the mittens?
What are you wearing now?

el
plumífero

las botas

los
pantalones cortes

la falda

las bragas

la
camiseta

la pinza

los zapatos

el mono

la camisa

el abrigo

la corbata

las medias

¿Qué llevas cuando hace frío?
¿Qué llevas cuando hace color?
¿De qué color son los guantes?
¿Qué llevas ahora?

La Familia

la bisabuela   el bisabuelo

la abuela   el abuelo   la bistía   el bistío

el padre   la madre   la tía   el tío

la hermana   el Osito   el hermano   la prima   los gemelos

Do you have any brothers or sisters?
How many brothers does Teddy Bear have?
How are you feeling now?
Are you scared of spiders?

Los Sentimientos

asustada

contento

tímido

desconcierta

aburrido

enfadado

pensativo

triste

orgulloso

arrepentido

¿Tienes hermanos o hermanas?
¿Cuántos hermanos tiene el Osito?
¿Qué tal?
¿Tienes miedo de las arañas?

La Fruta

 la pera

 el plátano

 la sandía

 la lima

la frambuesa

las uvas

el vaccinio

el higo

el mango

el ruibarbo

la uva espina

Which is your favorite fruit?
How many bananas can you see?
What is Teddy Bear holding?
Which fruits are red?

la naránja

el melocotón

el limón

la ciruela

el albaricoque

la cereza

la manzana

la papaya

el pomelo

la fresa

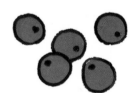
la grosella roja

la mandarina

la piña

¿Cuál es tu fruta preferida?
¿Cuántos plátanos hay?
¿Qué lleva el Osito?
¿Cuáles de las frutas son rojas?

75

Los Legumbres

los champiñones

la zanahoria

el brécol

el pimiento rojo

los guisantes

los puerros

la maíz

la cebolla

la patata

la coliflor

el tomate

el apio

Do you like carrots?
What is Teddy Bear eating?
Which vegetables are green?
What is your favorite vegetable?

la lechuga

la remolacha

las judías

la chirivía

el pepino

el rabaño

la batata

las judías verdes

el nabo

las hierbas

la col

el pepinito

¿A ti, te gusta las zanahorias?
¿Qué come el Osito?
¿Cuáles de los legumbres son verdes?
¿Cuál es tu legumbre preferido?

Las Flores

 la amapola   el lirio    la magarita   la campanula

el pensamiento

la narciso

la dalia

la girasol

el clavel

la azucena

la rosa

Which flowers are yellow?
Which flower grows very tall?
What is under the cup?
What is Teddy Bear holding?

¡A Comer!

la cucharilla

el pimiento

la sal

el platillo

la taza

¿Cuáles de las flores son amarillos?
¿Cuál de las flores crece muy alto?
¿Qué hay debajo de la taza?
¿Qué tiene el Osito en su mano?

el plato

el cuchillo

el tenedor

la cucharilla

el salvamanteles

el vaso

el cántarro

Las Palabras Opuestas

lento

rápido

grande

pequeño

alto

bajo

abierto

cerrado

puesto

apagado

abajo

arriba

Is an elephant small?
Is this book open or closed?
Are you inside or outside?
Are balloons heavy?

arriba   abajo   viejo   nuevo

lleno   vacío   ligero   pesado

dentro   fuera   delgado   gordo

¿Es pequeño el elefante?
¿Es abierto o cerrado el libro?
¿Estás a dentro o a fuera?
¿Están pesados, los globos?

Las Pájaros

el huevo

el pico

el ala

la pluma

el nido

el búho

el frailecillo

el tucán

el pingüino

el pavoreal

el avestruz

el emú

What is in the nest?
How many beaks can you see?
Which birds are black and white?
Which birds are eating fishes?

el martín pescador

la golondrina

el kiwi

el colbrí

el albatros

el buitre

la oca

el pavo

el flamenco

el pelícano

la cigüeña

el cisne

¿Qué hay en el nido?
¿Cuántos picos hay?
¿Cuáles de los pájaros son blancos y negros?
¿Cuáles de los pájaros comen el pescado?

Los Insectos

y otros animales pequeños

 la abeja
 el caracol
 la mariquita
 la lagartija

 el gusano

 la mariposa

 la avispa

 la oruga

 el escarabajo

 el milpiés

 el camaleón

Which minibeasts have wings?
Which minibeasts has six black spots?
Which minibeasts carries its own house?
Which minibeasts do not have legs?

 la mariposa nocturna

 la hormiga

 el saltamontes

 la babosa

 la mosca

 la pulga

 la crisálida

 el insecto de palo

 la tarántula

 el sapo

 el ciempiés

 la libélula

 la araña

¿Cuáles de los insectos tienen las alas?
¿Cuál tiene seis puntos negros?
¿Cuál lleva su propia casa?
¿Cuáles no tienen piernas?

Los Animales

la coala

el rinoceronte

el armadillo

el canguro

el oso polar

el gorila

la jirafa

el mono

el tigre

el elefante

la serpiente

el panda

Which animal is very tall?
Which animal is very big?
Which animal is Teddy Bear feeding?
Which is your favorite animal?

el mapache   el bisonte   el puerco espín   la cebra

el oso   el cocodrilo   el camello   el león

el cobo   el leopardo   el castor   el hipopótamo

¿Cuál de los animales es muy alto?
¿Cuál de los animales es muy grande?
¿El Osito da la comida a cuál de los animales?
¿Cuál es tu animal preferido?

Los Animales Domésticos

la casa del perro   el gatito   el hámster   la conejera

el canario

el conejo

el loro

el periquito

el conejo de indias

la comida de peces

el pez de colores

Do you have a pet?
Who lives in a doghouse?
Where is the rabbit?
What is in the fish tank?

 el cachorro

 las burbujas

 la escoba

 la tortuga

 el hueso

 la traílla

 el cuello

 el tazón de perro

 la cesta del gato

 el tanque

 la puerta de gatos

 la tortuga marina

 el tazón de agua

¿Tienes animales en casa?
¿Quién vive en la casa del perro?
¿Dónde está el conejo?
¿Qué hay en el tanque?

La Lista de Palabras

a

abacus *el ábaco*
adhesive bandage *la tirita*
airplane *el avión*
airport bus *el autobús*
alarm clock *el reloj*
albatross *el albatros*
alphabet *el alfabeto*
anchor *la áncora*
angry *enfadado*
animals *los animales*
ankle *el tobillo*
ant *la hormiga*
antenna *el aéreo*
apple *la manzana*
apricot *el albaricoque*
aquarium *la pecera*
archery *el tiro con arco*
arm *el brazo*
armadillo *el armadillo*
armchair *la butaca*
armoire *el armario*
armor *la armadura*
arrivals board *las llegadas*
aunt *la tía*
auto carrier *la transportadora de coches*

b

baby alarm *el monitor*
baby blanket *el chal*
baby bottle *el biberón*
baby carriage *el cochecito*
baby record book *el libro de bébé*
back *la espalda*
back brush *el cepillo de espalda*
backpack *la mochila*
baked beans *las judías asadas*
bakery *la panadería*
ball *la pelota*
balloon *el globo*
banana *el plátano*
bandage *la venda*
bank (piggy) *la hucha*
banjo *el banjo*
banner *la bandana*
bar code *el código*
baseball *el béisbol*
basket *la cesta*
basketball *el baloncesto*
bathing suit *el bañador*
bath mat *la estera de baño*
bathrobe *el batín*
bathtub *el baño*
beachball *la pelota*
beach umbrella *la sombrilla*
beads *el collar*
beak *el pico*
bear *el oso*
beaver *el castor*
bed *la cama*
bee *la abeja*
beet *la remolacha*
beetle *el escarabajo*
bench *el banco*
bib *el babero*
bicycle *la bicicleta*
bicycling *el ciclismo*
big *grande*
binoculars *los gemelos*
bird *el pájaro*
birdbath *el baño de pájaros*
bird feeder *la mesita de pájaros*
birdhouse *el nido*

birthday cake *la tarta*
birthday card *la tarjeta*
black *negro*
blanket *la manta*
blindfold *la venda*
blocks *los cubos*
blouse *la blusa*
blue *azul*
bluebell *la campanula*
blueberries *el vaccinio*
board book *el libro de cartón*
board game *el juego*
bone *el hueso*
bookcase *la estantería*
bootees *las botas de lana*
boots *las botas*
bored *aburrido*
bottles *las botellas*
bottom (body) *el trasero*
bottom (position) *abajo*
bow *el lazo*
bowling *el juego de bolos*
bow tie *la corbata de lazo*
branch *la rama*
bread *el pan*
bricks *los ladrillos*
bridge *el puente*
briefcase *la maleta*
broccoli *el brécol*
broom *la escoba*
brother *el hermano*
brown *marrón*
brush *el cepillo*
bubble bath *el jabón de baño*
bubbles *las burbujas*
bucket *el cubo*

buffalo *el bisonte*
bulldozer *la escavadora*
bulletin board *el tablón de anuncios*
buoy *la boya*
bus *el autocár*
bush *el arbusto*
butter *la mantequilla*
butterfly *la mariposa*
button *el botón*

c

cabbage *la col*
cabinet *el armario*
cage *la jaula*
cake *el pastel*
calendar *el calendario*
calf *el ternero*
camel *el camello*
camera *la máquina de fotos*
campfire *la hoguera*
camper *la caravana*
canary *el canario*
candle *la vela*
candy *los caramelos*
candy store *la bombonería*
cane *el bastón*
canister *el tarro*
canoe *la canoa*
cans *las latas*
car *el coche*
cardboard box *el cartón*
carnation *el clavel*
carpet *la maqueta*
carrot *la zanahoria*
carton *el cartón*
cashier *el cajero*
cash register *la caja*
cassette player *el estéreo personal*

castle *el castillo*
cat *el gato*
cat basket *la cesta del gato*
cat flap *la puerta de gatos*
caterpillar *la oruga*
cauliflower *la coliflor*
celery *el apio*
cello *el violoncelo*
centipede *el ciempiés*
cereal *los cereales*
chain *la cadena*
chalk *la tiza*
chalkboard *la pizarra*
chameleon *el cameleón*
change purse *el monedero*
changing mat *el colchón de cambiante*
check-in *el puente de control*
checks *los cuadrados*
cheek *la cara*
cheese *el queso*
cherry *la cereza*
chest of drawers *la cómoda*
chicks *los pollitos*
chimney *la chimenea*
chocolate *el chocolate*
chrysalis *la crisálida*
circle *el circulo*
cleaner *la limpiadora*
climbing (sport) *la escaleda*
clipboard *el tablón*
cloak *la capa*
clock *el reloj*
cloth book *el libro de tela*
clothespin *la pinza*
cloud *el nube*
clown *el payaso*
coat *el abrigo*

coat hook *la percha*
coffee *el café*
cold *el frío*
collar *el cuello*
colored pencils *las pinturas*
coloring book *el libro de colores*
comb *el peine*
comforter *la colcha*
comic book *el tebeo*
computer *el ordenador*
conductor *el director*
container ship *el buque*
control tower *la torre de control*
conveyor belt *la cinta transportadora*
cookbook *el libro de cocina*
cookie *la galleta*
cookies *las galletas*
coral *el coral*
corn *la maíz*
cotton balls *el algodón*
counter *la tabla*
cousin *la prima*
cow *la vaca*
crab *el cangrejo*
cradle *la cuna*
crane *la grúa*
crawling *gatear*
crayons *los coloretes*
crib *la camita*
cricket *el criquet*
crocodile *el cocodrilo*
crown *la corona*
cucumber *el pepino*
cuddling *abrazar*
cup *la copa*
curtain *la cortina*
cymbals *los platillos*

d

daffodil *la narciso*
dahlia *la dalia*
daisy *la magarita*
dancing *bailar*
deck chair *la tumbona*
decorations *los adornos*
delivery van *la furgoneta*
dew *el rocío*
diamond *el diamante*
diaper *el pañal*
diaper bag *el bolso de bébés*
dice *los dados*
dish towel *el trapo de cocina*
dishwasher *el lava platos*
dishwashing liquid *jabón de fregar*
diver *el saltador*
doctor *el médico*
dog *el perro*
dog bowl *el tazón de perro*
doghouse *la casa del perro*
doll *la muñeca*
dollhouse *la casa de muñecas*
dolphin *el delfín*
door *la puerta*
doorbell *el timbre*
doorknob *el pomo de puerta*
doorstep *el umbral*
dots *los puntos*
doughnuts *los churros*
down *abajo*
dragon *el dragón*
dragonfly *la libélula*
drain *la boca de alcantarilla*
drainboard *el escurreplatos*
drawer *el cajón*

dressing *poner la ropa*
dressing-up costume *la disfraz*
dressmaker's dummy *el maniquí*
drill *el taladero*
drinking *beber*
driver *el conductor*
driveway *la calzada*
drying *secarse*
duck *el pato*
duckling *el patito*
dump truck *el carro*
dust cloth *el trapo de polvo*

e

ear *la oreja*
easel *el caballete*
eating *comer*
egg *el huevo*
eight *ocho*
eighteen *dieciocho*
elbow *el codo*
elephant *el elefante*
elevator *el ascensor*
eleven *once*
elf *el elfo*
embarrassed *desconcierta*
empty *vacío*
emu *el emú*
envelope *el sobre*
eraser *la goma*
eye patch *el pedazo del ojo*
eye *el ojo*
eyebrow *la ceja*

f

fairy *el hada*
fall *el otoño*
farmer *el granjero*
farmhouse *la granja*
fast *rápido*
fat *gordo*
father *el padre*

faucet *el grifo*
feather *la pluma*
felt-tip pens *los rotuladores*
fence *la valla*
field *el campo*
fifteen *quince*
fig *el higo*
finger *el dedo*
fireplace *la chimenea*
first *primero*
fish *la pez*
fish food *la comida de peces*
fish tank *el tanque*
fisherman *el pescador*
fishing boat *el barco pescadero*
fishing net *la red*
fishing rod *la caña*
five *cinco*
flag *la bandera*
flamingo *el flamenco*
flashlight *la lámpara de bolsillo*
flea *la pulga*
flight attendant *la azafata*
flippers *las aletas*
flood *la inundación*
flour *la harina*
flower bed *el macizo de flores*
flowerpot *la maceta*
flowers *las flores*
flute *la flauta*
fly *la mosca*
foal *el potro*
fog *la niebla*
food mixer *la mezcladora*
foot *el pie*
football *el fútbol americano*
fork (garden) *la horca*
fork (table) *el tenedor*
fort *el castillo*
fountain *la fuente*
four *cuatro*

fourteen *catorce*
fries *las patatas fritas*
frog *el sapo*
frost *la helada*
fruit *la fruta*
frying pan *el sartén*
full *lleno*

g

galleon *el galeón*
garbage truck *el furgón de basura*
gate *la puerta de verja*
get-well card *la tarjeta*
giant *el gigante*
giraffe *la jirafa*
glass *el vaso*
glove *el guante*
goggles *los anteojos*
go-cart *el gokart*
goldfish *el pez de colores*
golf *el golf*
goose *la oca*
gorilla *el gorila*
grandfather *el abuelo*
grandmother *la abuela*
grapefruit *el pomelo*
grapes *las uvas*
grass *la césped*
grasshopper *el saltamontes*
gray *gris*
great-aunt *la bistía*
great-grandfather *el bisabuelo*
great-grandmother *la bisabuela*
great-uncle *el bistío*
green *verde*
green beans *las judías verdes*
guinea pig *el conejo de indias*
guitar *la guitarra*

gymnastics *la gimnasia*

h

hair *el pelo*
hairbrush *el cepillo*
hamburger *la hamburguesa*
hammer *el martillo*
hamster *el hámster*
hand fork *la horca del mano*
hand *la mano*
handkerchief *el panuelo*
hand puppet *el títere*
hangar *el hangar*
hanger *la percha*
hanging basket *la cesta de plantas*
happy *contento*
harbor *el puerto*
harp *la harpa*
hat *el sombrero*
head *la cabeza*
heart *la corazón*
heat *el calor*
heavy *pesado*
hedge *el seto*
height chart *la tabla de estatura*
helicopter *el helicoptero*
hen *la gallina*
herbs *las hierbas*
high chair *la silla alta*
high jump *la salta alta*
hiker *el paseante*
hill *la colina*
hippopotamus *el hipopótamo*
hoe *la azada*
honey *la miel*
hook *el gancho*
hoop *el arco*
hopping *saltar*
horn *la sirena*
horse *el caballo*

hose *la manga*
hotdog *el perrito caliente*
hummingbird *el colibrí*
hundred *cien*
hurricane *el ventarrón*
hutch *la conejera*
hypodermic needle *la jeringa*

l

ice *el helado*
ice cream *el helado*
ice pop *el helado*
ice skates *los botes del patinaje*
ice skating *el patinaje*
icicles *los carámbanos*
inside *dentro*
iris *el lirio*
iron *la plancha*
iron fence *la verja*
island *la isla*

j

jacket *la chaqueta*
Jack-in-the-box *la caja sorpresa*
jars *los tarros*
jeans *los vaqueros*
jellyfish *la medusa*
jetty *el embarcadero*
jogger *el corredor*
judo *el judo*
juice *el zumo*
jumping *saltar*
jumping rope *saltar*
jumprope *la cuerda de saltar*

k

kangaroo *el canguro*
kettle *el calentador de agua*

kettledrums *los tímpanos*

keyboard *el teclado de música*

keyhole *el agujero de llave*

keys *las llaves*

kicking *dar un puntapié*

king *el rey*

kingfisher *el martín pescador*

kite *la cometa*

kitten *el gatito*

kiwi *el kiwi*

knee pads *la rodillera*

knee *la rodilla*

knife *el cuchillo*

knight *el caballero*

koala *la coala*

l

label *la etiqueta*

ladder *la escalera*

ladybug *la mariquita*

lake *el lago*

lamb *la oveja*

lamp *la lámpara*

lance *la lanza*

lawn mower *el cortacesped*

leash *la traílla*

leaves *los hojas*

leek *los puerros*

leg *la pierna*

lemon *el limón*

leopard *el leopardo*

lettuce *la lechuga*

life jacket *el chaleco salvavidas*

life preserver *la guindola*

light bulb *la bombilla*

light *la luz*

light (weight) *ligero*

lighthouse *el faro*

lightning *el relámpago*

lily *la azucena*

lima beans *las judías*

lime *la lima*

line *la cola*

lion *el león*

lips *los labios*

litter basket *la papelera*

little *pequeño*

lizard *la lagatija*

lobster *la langosta*

lobster pot *la langostera*

log *los troncos*

lollipop *el pirulí*

luggage cart *el caro*

lunch box *la caja de comida*

m

magazine *la revista*

magician *el mágico*

mallet *el mazo*

mango *el mango*

map *el mapa*

maracas *las maracas*

marbles *las carnicas*

mask *la máscara*

mast *el mástil*

mattress *el colchón*

meadow *el campo*

measuring tape *el metro*

medicine *la medicina*

mermaid *la sirena*

message in a bottle *el mensaje de botella*

microwave *la micro-onda*

milk *la leche*

milkshake *el batido*

millipede *el milpiés*

mirror *el espejo*

mittens *los guantes*

mixing bowl *la escudilla*

mobile *el pendiente*

modeling clay *la arcilla*

money *el dinero*

monkey *el mono*

mop *el fregasuelos*

moth *la mariposa nocturna*

mother *la madre*

motorboat *el barco de motor*

motorcycle *la moto*

mountain *la montaña*

mouse *la rata*

mouth *la boca*

moving van *el furgón*

muffin *el pastel*

mug *la taza*

mushrooms *los champiñones*

music *la música*

music stand *el atril*

n

nail brush *el cepillo*

nails *los clavos*

napkin *la servilleta*

navy *azul oscurro*

nest *el nido*

new *nuevo*

newspaper *el periódico*

nightgown *el camisón*

night table *la mesita de noche*

nine *nueve*

nineteen *diecinueve*

Noah's ark *la Arca de Noé*

nose *la nariz*

notebook *el cuaderno*

notes *las notas*

nurse *la enfermera*

nuts *las nueces*

o

oboe *el oboe*

ocean *el mar*

ocean liner *el transatlántico*

octopus *el pulpo*

off (lamp) *apagado*

old *viejo*

omelet *la tortilla*

on (lamp) *puesto*

one *uno (una)*

onion *la cebolla*

open *abierto*

orange (colour) *naranja*

orange (fruit) *la naránja*

ostrich *el avestruz*

outside *fuera*

oval *la ovalada*

overalls *el mono*

owl *el búho*

oyster *la ostra*

p

pacifier *el chupete*

package *el paquete*

paddle *el canalete*

page boy *el paje*

paint *el bote de pintura*

paintbox *las pinturas*

paintbrush *el pincel*

painting *el dibujo*

pajamas *el pijama*

palm *la palma*

palm tree *la palmera*

panda *el panda*

pansy *el pensamiento*

pants *los pantalones*

papaya *la papya*

paper *el papel*

paper cup *la taza de papel*

parachute *el paracaída*

parakeet *el periquito*

parka *el plumífero*

parrot *el loro*

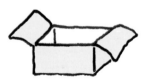

parsnip   *la chirivía*
party bag   *el bolsito de fiesta*
party dress   *el vestido*
party hat   *el sombrero de fiesta*
path   *la senda*
paw   *la pata*
peach   *el melocotón*
peacock   *el pavoreal*
pear   *la pera*
pearl   *la perla*
peas   *los guisantes*
pebbles   *las pierdrecitas*
pedal car   *el coche*
pelican   *el pelícano*
penguin   *el pingüino*
penknife   *la navaja*
pepper   *el pimiento*
photograph   *la foto*
piano   *el piano*
pick-up truck   *el camión de averías*
picnic   *el picnic*
picnic basket   *el cesto*
picture   *la obra*
picture frame   *el cuadro*
pie   *la tarta*
piece of cake   *la ración de la tarta*
pig   *el cerdo*
pigeon   *la paloma*
piggy bank   *la hucha*
piglet   *el cerdito*
pillow (bed)   *la almohada*
pillow (chair)   *el cojín*
pilot   *el piloto*
pineapple   *la piña*
pink   *rosa*
pipe   *el caño*
pirate   *el pirata*
pirate flag   *la bandera de pirata*
pistol   *la pistola*
pitcher   *el jarro*
pizza   *la pizza*

place mat   *el salvamanteles*
plank   *el tablón*
plant   *la planta*
plaster cast   *la escayola*
plate   *el plato*
playhouse   *la casa de muñecas*
pliers   *los alicates*
plum   *la ciruela*
pocket   *el bolsillo*
polar bear   *el oso blanco*
pole vaulting   *el salto con pértiga*
pond   *el estanque*
poppy   *la amapola*
porcupine   *el puerco espín*
porter   *el portero*
porthole   *la portilla*
portrait ·   *el dibujo*
poster   *el póster*
potato   *la patata*
potty   *el orinal*
power shovel   *la escavadora*
present   *el regalo*
prince   *el príncipe*
princess   *la princesa*
proud   *orgulloso*
puddles   *los charcos*
puffin   *el frailecillo*
pull toy   *la jugueta de bébés*
pulling   *tirar*
pumpkin   *la calabaza*
pupil   *el alumno*
puppy   *el cachorro*
purple   *violeta*
purse   *el bolso*
pushing   *empujar*
puzzle   *el rompecabezas*

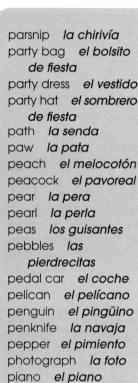

q

queen   *la reina*

r

rabbit   *el conejo*
raccoon   *el mapache*
racing car   *el coche de carreras*
radio   *la radio*
radishes   *el rabaño*
railroad track   *la vía*
rain   *la lluvia*
rainbow   *el arco de iris*
rake   *el rastrillo*
raspberry   *la frambuesa*
rattle   *el sonajero*
reading   *leer*
receipt   *el recibo*
recorder   *la flauta de pico*
rectangle   *el rectangulo*
red   *rojo*
red pepper   *el pimiento rojo*
refrigerator   *el frigorifico*
remote control   *el tele control*
restrooms   *los servicios*
rhinoceros   *el rhinoceronte*
rhubarb   *el ruibarbo*
ribbon   *la cinta*
rice   *el arroz*
riding (a bicycle)   *montar la bicicleta*
river   *el río*
robot   *el robot*
rocket   *el cohete*
rocking chair   *la mecedora*
rocking horse   *el caballo de balancín*
rocks   *las rocas*
roller skating   *el patinaje de ruedas*
roller skates   *los patines*
rolling pin   *el rodillo de cocina*
roof   *el tejado*
roof tile   *la teja*
rooster   *el gallo*
rope   *la cuerda*
rose   *la rosa*
rowing   *el piragüismo*
rowboat   *el bote de remos*
rubber duck   *el pato*
rubber tube   *el aro de goma*
rug   *la alfombra*
ruler   *la regla*
running   *correr*
runway   *la pista de aterrizaje*

s

sack race   *la carrera de bolsas*
sad   *triste*
safety helmet   *el casco*
sailboat   *el barco de yate*
salad   *la ensalada*
salesclerk   *la dependienta*
salt   *la sal*
sand   *la arena*
sandbox   *el hoyo de arena*
sandcastle   *el castillo de arena*
sandpaper   *el papel de lija*
sandwiches   *los bocadillos*
saucepan   *la cacerola*
saucer   *el platillo*
sauce   *la salsa*
sausage   *la salchicha*
saw   *la sierra*
saxophone   *el saxafón*
scale   *la balanza*

scarecrow *el espanta pájaros*
scared *asustada*
scarf *la bufunda*
school *el colegio*
schoolbag *el bolso*
scissors *las tijeras*
scooter *el patinete*
screwdriver *el destornillador*
screws *los tornillos*
sea gull *la gaviota*
sea shell *la concha de mar*
seahorse *el caballito de mar*
seaweed *las algas*
second *segundo*
security light *la luz de seguridad*
seeds *las semillas*
seesaw *el subibaja*
seven *siete*
seventeen *diecisiete*
sewing machine *la máquina de coser*
shampoo *el champú*
shark *el tiburón*
shears *las tijeras de jardín*
shed *el cobertizo*
sheep *la cordera*
sheet *la sabana*
shelf *el estante*
shield *el escudo*
shirt *la camisa*
shoes *los zapatos*
shoe store *la zapatería*
shopper *el comprador*
shopping bag *la bolsa*
shopping cart *el carro*
short *bajo*
shorts *los pantalones cortes*
shoulder *el hombro*
shower *la ducha*

shower curtain *la cortina de ducha*
shut *cerrado*
shy *tímido*
sidewalk *la acera*
sign *el signo*
singing *cantar*
sink *el fregadero*
sister *la hermana*
sitting *sentar*
six *seis*
sixteen *dieciseis*
skateboard *el mono patín*
skirt *la falda*
skis *el patín*
skylight *el tragaluz*
sled *el trineo*
sleeper *la camiseta de dormir*
sleeping *dormir*
sleeping bag *el saco de dormir*
slide *el tobogán*
sling *el cabestrillo*
slippers *las zapatillas*
slow *lento*
slug *la babosa*
snail *el caracol*
snake *la serpiente*
sneakers *las zapatillas de deporte*
snow *la nieve*
snowflake *el copo de nieve*
snowman *el hombre de nieve*
soap *el jabón*
soccer *el fútbol*
socks *los calcetines*
soda pop *la gaseosa*
sofa *el sofá*
soft toy *el juguete mimosa*
soil *la tierra*
soldiers *los solditos*
sorry *arrepentido*
soup *la sopa*
spade *la pala*

spaghetti *los espaguetis*
spider *la araña*
spider web *la telaraña*
sponge *la esponja*
spoon *la cucharilla*
spring *la primervera*
square *el cuadro*
squirrel *la ardilla*
stacking cups *las tazitas*
standing *esperar*
star *la estrella*
starfish *la estrella de mar*
steamroller *la apisonadora*
stereo *el estéreo*
stethoscope *el estetoscopio*
stomach *el estómago*
stool *el taburete*
stork *la cigüeña*
stove *la cocina eléctrica*
straw *la pajita*
strawberry *la fresa*
streamer *la guirnalda de papel*
street *la calle*
streetlight *la farola*
street sign *el poste indicador*
stripes *las rayas*
stroller *la silleta*
submarine *el submarino*
sugar *el azúcar*
suitcase *la maleta*
summer *el verano*
sun *el sol*
sunflower *la girasol*
sunglasses *las gafas de sol*
sun hat *el sombrero de paja*
sunscreen *la crema bronceadora*

sunshine *el sol*
swallow *la golondrina*
swan *el cisne*
sweater *el suéter*
sweet potato *la batata*
swimmer *el nadador*
swimming *la natación*
swimming trunks *el traje de baño*
swing *los columpios*
sword *la espada*

✝

table *la mesa*
tablecloth *el mantel*
tall *alto*
tambourine *la pandereta*
tandem *el tándem*
tangerine *la mandarina*
tanker *el camión de gasolina*
tarantula *la tarántula*
tea set *el servicio de té*
teacher *la profesora*
team *el equipo*
teaspoon *la cucharilla*
teething ring *el chupador*
telephone *el teléfono*
television *la televisión*
temperature chart *la tabla de temperatura*
ten *diez*
tennis *el tenis*
tent *las tiendas de campaña*
thermometer *el termómetro*
Thermos *el termo*
thin *delgado*
third *tecero*
thirteen *trece*

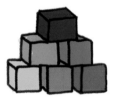

thoughtful *pensativo*
three *tres*
three-legged race *la carrera de tres piernas*
thumb *el pulgar*
tickets *los billetes*
tie *la corbata*
tiger *el tigre*
tights *las medias*
tissues *el tisú*
toadstool *el hongo*
toaster *el tostador*
toe *el dedo de pie*
toilet *el váter*
toilet paper *el papel higiénico*
tomato *el tomate*
tool box *la caja de herramientas*
toothbrush *el cepillo de dientes*
toothpaste *la pasta de dientes*
top (toy) *la peonza*
top (position) *arriba*
top hat *el sombrero de copa*
tornado *el tornado*
tortoise *la tortuga*
toucan *el tucán*
towel *la toalla*
toy boat *el barco*
toy box *el baúl*
tractor *el tractór*
tractor-trailer *el camión*
trailer *la caravana*
train car *el vagón*
train engine *el tren*
training cup *la tazita*
trampolining *el salto de trampolín*
trapdoor *la escotilla*
trash can *el cubo de basura*
tray *la bandeja*

treasure chest *el cajón*
treasure map *la mapa*
tree *el árbol*
trellis *la espaldera*
triangle (instrument) *el tríangulo*
triangle (shape) *el triangulo*
tricycle *el triciclo*
trombone *el trombón*
trophy *la copa*
trowel *la paleta*
truck *la furgoneta*
trumpet *la trompeta*
trunk *el tronco*
T-shirt *la camiseta*
turkey *el pavo*
turnip *el nabo*
turtle *la tortuga marina*
twelve *doce*
twenty *veinte*
twins *los gemelos*
two *dos*

u

uncle *el tío*
underpants *las bragas*
undershirt *la camiseta*
up *arriba*

v

vacuum cleaner *el aspirador*
vase *el vaso de flores*
vegetables *los legumbres*
vest *el chaleco*
video *el vídeo*
village *el pueblo*

vintage car *el coche clásico*
violin *el violín*
visitor *el visitante*
vulture *el buitre*

W

wagon *la caretilla*
walker *las muletas*
walking *andar*
walking stick *el insecto de palo*
wall tiles *los azulejos*
wallpaper *el papel de paredes*
wand *la varilla de virtudes*
washcloth *el paño*
washing *lavarse*
washstand *el lavabo*
wasp *la avispa*
wastebasket *la papelera*
watch *el reloj*
water glass *el vaso de agua*
water bowl *el tazón de agua*
waterfall *la cascada*
watering can *la regadera*
watermelon *la sandía*
water-skier *el esquiador acuatico*
water wings *los brazales*
waves *las olas*
waving *agitar el brazo*
weightlifting *el levantamiento de pesos*
wet suit *el traje de baño*
whale *la ballena*

wheelbarrow *la carretilla*
wheelchair *la silla de ruedas*
wheels *las ruedas*
white *blanco*
wind *el viento*
window *la ventana*
window box *la jardinera de ventana*
windsock *la mango*
wing *el ala*
winter *el invierno*
wishing well *el fuente de deseos*
wolf *el cobo*
wooden spoon *la cuchara de palo*
woods *el bosque*
workbench *la mesa de trabajo*
worm *el gusano*
wrapping paper *el papel*
wrench *la llave de tuercas*
wrist *la muñeca*
writing *escribir*

X

xylophone *el xilofón*

y

yard *el jardín*
yellow *amarillo*
yogurt *el yogur*
yo-yo *el yoyo*

z

zebra *la cebra*
zigzags *los zig zag*
zucchini *el pepinito*